IF WE EVER BREAK UP, THIS IS MY BOOK

IF WE EVER BREAK UP, THIS IS MY BOOK

BY JASON LOGAN

~ SIMON SPOTLIGHT ENTERTAINMENT ~

NEW YORK LONDON TORONTO SYDNEY

SSE

SIMON SPOTLIGHT ENTERTAINMENT
AN IMPRINT OF SIMON & SCHUSTER
1230 AVENUE OF THE AMERICAS, NEW YORK, NEW YORK 10020
COPYRIGHT © 2005 BY JASON LOGAN
ALL RIGHTS RESERVED, INCLUDING THE RIGHT OF REPRODUCTION
IN WHOLE OR IN PART IN ANY FORM.
SIMON SPOTLIGHT ENTERTAINMENT AND RELATED LOGOS
ARE TRADEMARKS OF SIMON & SCHUSTER, INC.
MANUFACTURED IN THE UNITED STATES OF AMERICA
FIRST EDITION
10 9 8 7 6 5 4 3 2 1
THE LIBRARY OF CONGRESS CATALOGING-IN-PUBLICATION
DATA HAS BEEN REQUESTED FOR THIS TITLE.
ISBN-13: 978-1-4169-0825-8
ISBN-10: 1-4169-0825-0

*
ACTUALLY, THERE ARE MORE THAN A FEW THINLY VEILED
REFERENCES TO FORMER FRIENDS AND LOVERS, BUT I AM
HOPING THEY ARE OVER IT ENOUGH NOT TO SUE.

DEDICATION

FOR LOUISE
AND KATRINA
AND SHARY
AND HEIDI

Ex Libris

IF WE EVER BREAK UP,
DON'T FORGET THIS IS
MY BOOK

Name: _____

Date: _____

AUTHOR'S NOTE

NOT TO SPOIL THE ENDING
FOR YOU, BUT EVERYTHING
IS GOING TO BE OKAY.

CHOOSE

HOLD
ON

LET
GO

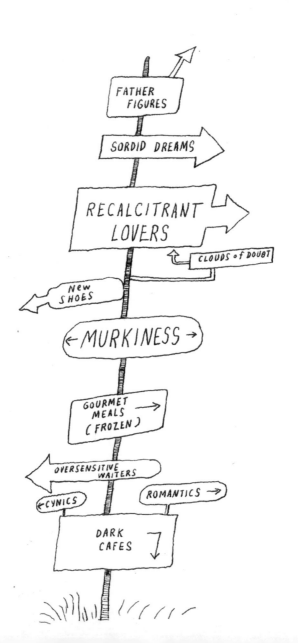

Signs of Trouble

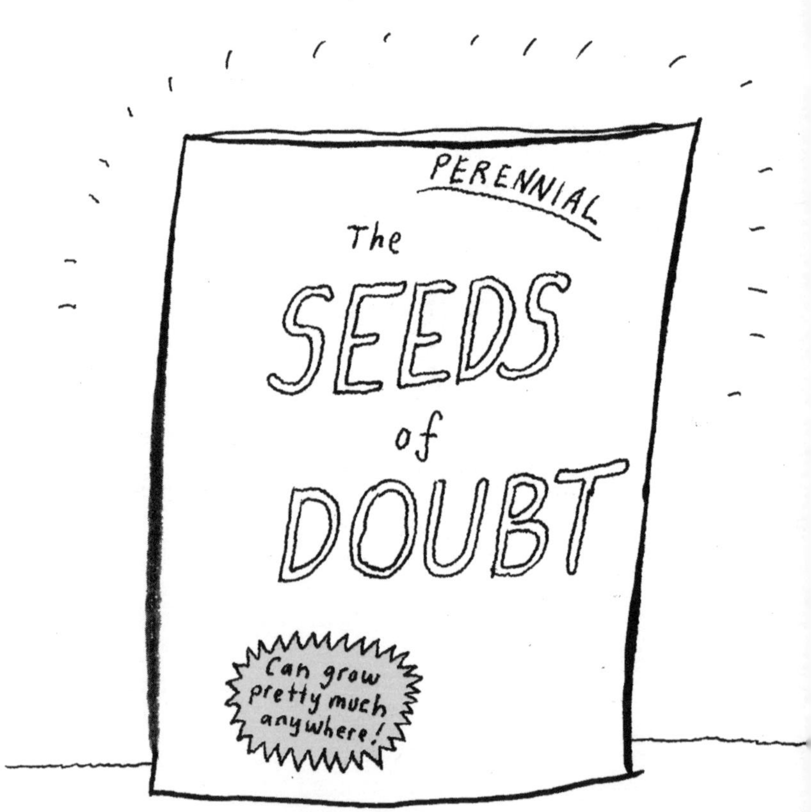
PERENNIAL
The SEEDS of DOUBT
Can grow pretty much anywhere!

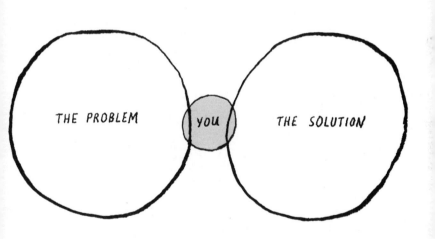

THE DISTANCE

YOU

UNMET
NEEDS

MISCOMMUNICATION

JEALOUSY ABOUT
THE CAT'S AFFECTIONS

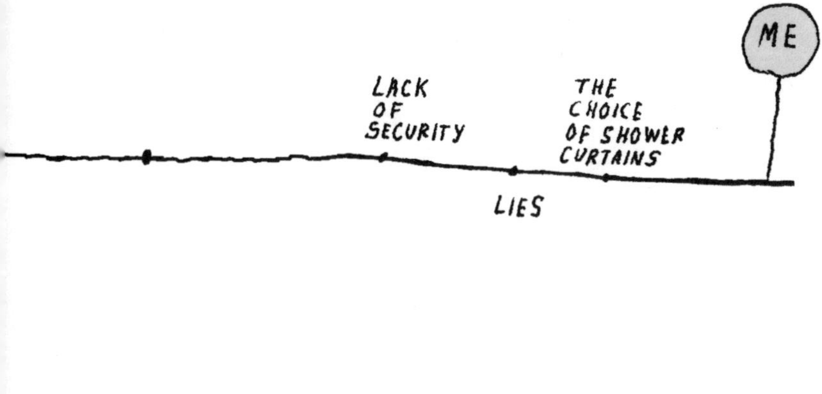
ME
LACK OF SECURITY
THE CHOICE OF SHOWER CURTAINS
LIES

YOUR MOOD

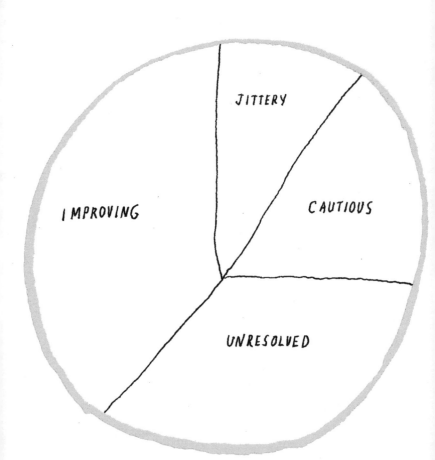

STRANGERS
ARE BEGINNING
TO NOTE THAT
YOUR CHOICES
ARE UNSOUND.

HIDING ACTIVITY

AVOID THOSE
PEOPLE YOU
HAVE NOTHING
LEFT TO SAY TO

STORMING OUT

(HOW TO PACK)

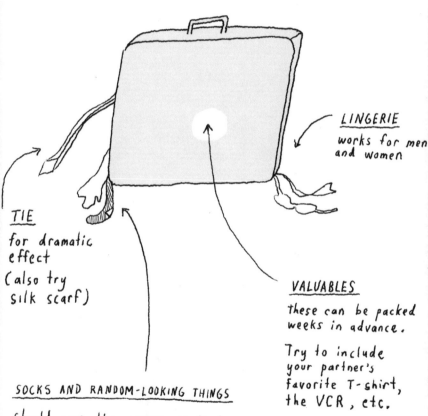

LINGERIE
works for men
and women

TIE
for dramatic
effect
(also try
silk scarf)

VALUABLES
these can be packed
weeks in advance.

Try to include
your partner's
favorite T-shirt,
the VCR, etc.

SOCKS AND RANDOM-LOOKING THINGS
Should give the appearance that
you just stuffed some things in
a suitcase five minutes ago.

TRYING TO BE POSITIVE
ABOUT THE HAPPY PEOPLE

You're on your own
for this one. Sorry

CRISIS ACTIVITY

1. THINK OF SOMETHING DIFFICULT.
2. START CALLING IT YOUR CRISIS.

LET'S LET THAT PERCOLATE A LITTLE

MAGIC ACTIVITY

PRETEND THAT THE MAGIC
IS NOT GONE.

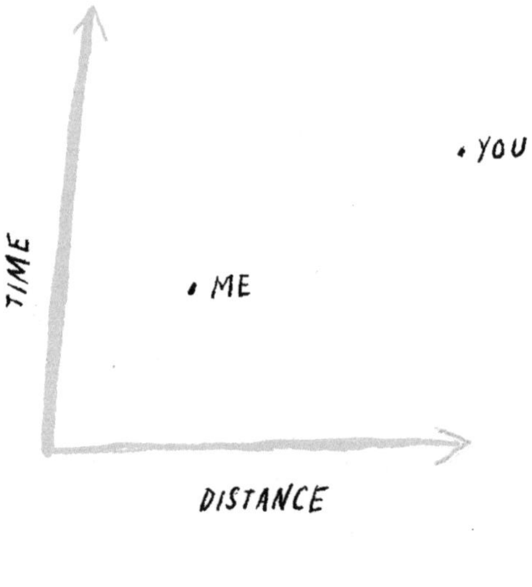
YOU
TIME
ME
DISTANCE

BECAUSE

☐ TODAY WAS A GOOD DAY

☐ I COULD

☐ YOU COULDN'T

☐ OF THAT METEOR SHOWER

UNEVENNESS

SOMETIMES
THINGS
ARE JUST
UNEVEN.

A SEEMINGLY SIMPLE MAZE

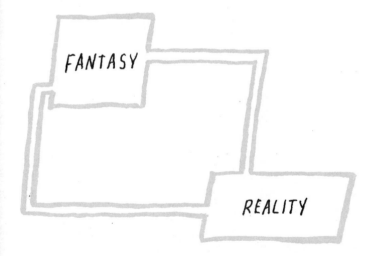

BELOW THE SURFACE

THE SURFACE

REGRET

THE DARK SUSPICION

BITTERNESS

ABANDONMENT

MELANCHOLY

LOVE

If he calls
looking for me,
tell him I am
out looking
for him.

GAVE OUT

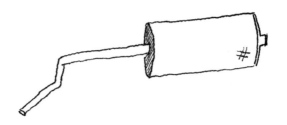

A LONG TIME AGO

YOUR EMOTIONS

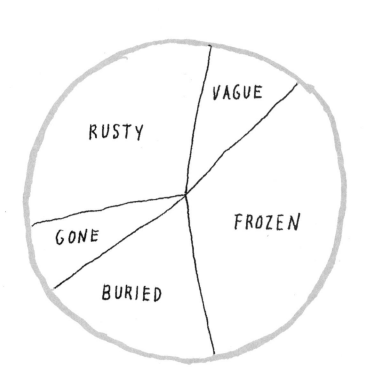

ANALOGY

like the whiff of
a good smell to a
mind too troubled
to really smell it...

not completely in love anymore?

HOW MANY OF THESE PESKY HABITS IRRITATE YOU?

- ○ CHOICE OF SOCK COLOR
- ○ METHOD OF WRAPPING PRESENTS FOR YOU
- ○ TONE OF VOICE USED ON PET
- ○ OVERWATERING PLANTS
- ○ NOTHING I CAN PUT MY FINGER ON, BUT I AM IRRITATED NONETHELESS
- ○ INABILITY TO WITHSTAND CONSTANT CRITICISM
- ○ TENDENCY OF HAIR TO FORM INTO A COWLICK
- ○ OVERFRIENDLINESS TOWARD YOUR PARENTS
- ○ HAT RARELY MATCHES SCARF
- ○ NOT UNDERSTANDING OR DEALING WITH YOUR UNSPOKEN CONCERNS
- ○ ASKING HOW YOU FEEL RATHER THAN JUST KNOWING HOW YOU FEEL

I WILL NEVER

☐ GROW A GOATEE

☐ FALL ASLEEP WHILE YOU
ARE TELLING ME YOUR DREAMS

☐ CONTRADICT YOUR EXAGGERATIONS

☐ CHANGE

NOW THAT YOU ARE GONE
I'M REMEMBERING THINGS
I WAS GOING TO SAY TO
IMPRESS YOU.

LAYING THE BLAME

I, _____, *blame* _____
for _____.

Please use space below for additional comments.

ITEMS THAT MAY BE USED IN MOMENTS OF GREAT CRISIS

GLASS OF WATER

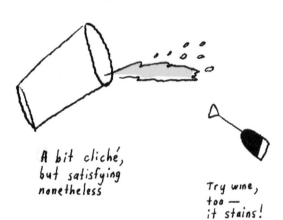

A bit cliché, but satisfying nonetheless

Try wine, too — it stains!

THE KITCHEN TABLE

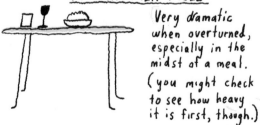

Very dramatic when overturned, especially in the midst of a meal. (you might check to see how heavy it is first, though.)

YOUR HAND

slapping is pretty much out of date now, but women are still allowed. Try to make a loud sound.

CHEAP CLOTHES-DRYING RACK

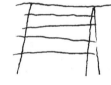

Inexpensive to replace, splinters nicely, and has a fairly dramatic effect

SPECIAL VASE

You may come to regret this when your parents visit and notice its absence.

NOW WHO THE HELL IS GONNA...

- ☐ WATER THE FERN
- ☐ TWIST THE TOPS OFF BOTTLES FOR ME
- ☐ CHANGE THE LIGHTBULBS — YOU KNOW THE LITTLE ONES WE KEEP ON THE VERY TOP SHELF

PLEASE DO NOT
SELL THIS AT
A GARAGE SALE
AFTER I AM GONE

The Really
Bad Period

Eating Alone

Have you tried those little half bottles of wine?

HOW ARE YOU FEELING TODAY?

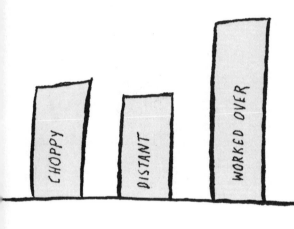

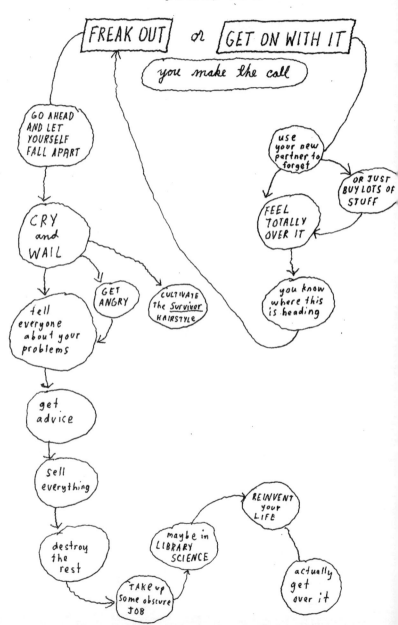

A SEED FROM
THE PLANT
THAT GREW FROM
THE ROOT OF
YOUR TROUBLES

Your First Encounter

Since when did she start wearing lipstick?
since when did he stop meeting my eyes?
since when did they start drinking Herbal tea?

THE PRIZES

1. WINNER TAKES ALL.

2. LOSER TAKES WHATEVER
   LITTLE THINGS ARE LEFT
   OVER THAT NO ONE ELSE
   WANTS.

SOME WINTER QUESTIONS FINALLY ANSWERED

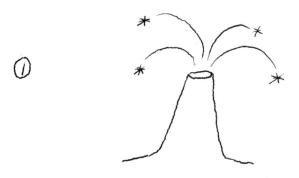

WHERE ALL THE SNOW COMES FROM

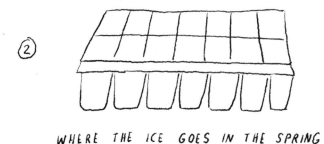

WHERE THE ICE GOES IN THE SPRING

WHERE YOUR HEART IS NOW

During This Difficult Time...

IT MIGHT BE BEST JUST NOT TO THINK ABOUT:

- [ ] THAT OLD BOX OF LETTERS
- [ ] THE DEATH OF CHILDHOOD PETS THAT — ADMITTEDLY — YOU WERE UNDERFEEDING
- [ ] THAT PLANNED TRIP TO MOROCCO
- [ ] THE LIFESTYLES OF THE VERY BEAUTIFUL
- [ ] ANYTHING TO DO WITH THE TELEPHONE

YOUR DARK THOUGHTS
APPEAR TO HAVE STARTED
A SMALL FAMILY.

SPIRALS!

(let's take a look)

THE SPIRAL OF PAIN

THE SPIRAL OF LOVE

THE SPIRAL OF CONFUSION

THE SPIRAL OF BLEAK THOUGHTS

THE SPIRAL OF
DIMINISHING CHARMS

THE SHORT-TERM
RELATIONSHIP SPIRAL

THE SPIRAL OF INCREASING
CHEESY ROMANTIC MOVIES

THE DECODER

THE PHRASE	ITS MEANING
I'VE ALWAYS WANTED TO CHECK OUT EUROPE ON MY OWN.	AND I BOUGHT A ONE-WAY TICKET.
IT'S NOT YOU.	OH, IT'S YOU ALRIGHT.
I JUST NEED SOME TIME TO FIGURE THINGS OUT.	THE FIRST THING TO FIGURE OUT IS HOW TO GET OUT WITHOUT HURTING YOUR FEELINGS.
I REALLY VALUE OUR FRIENDSHIP.	OUR SEX LIFE IS OVER.
I THINK YOU WILL MAKE SOMEONE VERY HAPPY.	GOOD LUCK TO YOU.
YOU CAN KEEP THE CAT.	I WILL BE KEEPING EVERYING ELSE.
DO YOU REMEMBER WHO BOUGHT THIS CD?	OTHERWISE, I'M COMPLETELY PACKED.
HOW DO YOU FEEL ABOUT OPEN RELATIONSHIPS?	BECAUSE YOU'RE IN ONE NOW.

The Showdown

INTERNALIZING THE
PAIN IS NO LONGER
JUST A PHRASE.

I AM PRETTY SURE

THAT THE WARMTH
YOU ARE FEELING
IS THE DIRECT RESULT
OF THE PHOTOGRAPHS
YOU HAVE LIT ON FIRE.

Your Second Encounter

so, how's the career going?
well, that would depend on whether you'd consider experimenting with medical marijuana as a career in the health sciences.

MAYBE A LITTLE TELEVISION
WILL HELP TAKE MY MIND OFF HIM
let's have a look at the menu

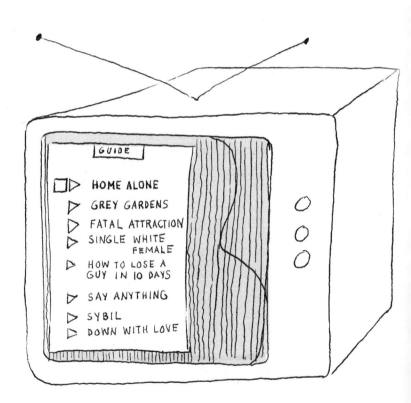

Express YOUR ANGER

BAD

SLIGHTLY BETTER

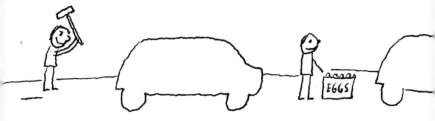

OLD NOTES

SEEM INFUSED WITH A KIND OF
BITTERSWEET TRANSCENDENCE
LEADING TO A DEEP DEPRESSION

RETAINING A MEASURE OF DIGNITY
IN THE FACE OF GREAT PAIN

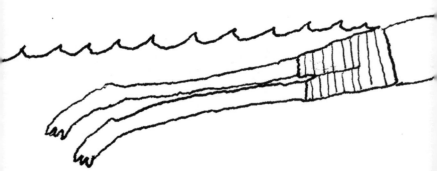

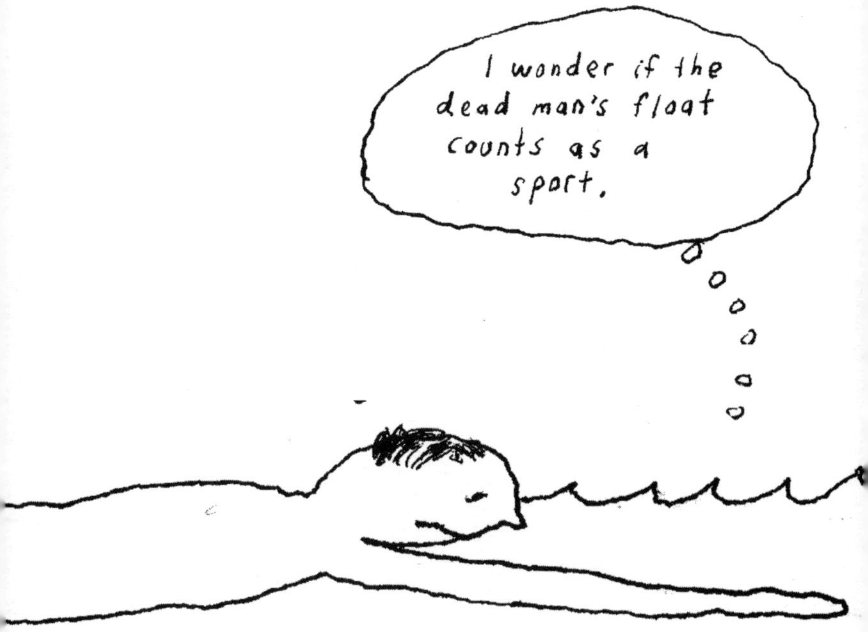
I wonder if the dead man's float counts as a sport.

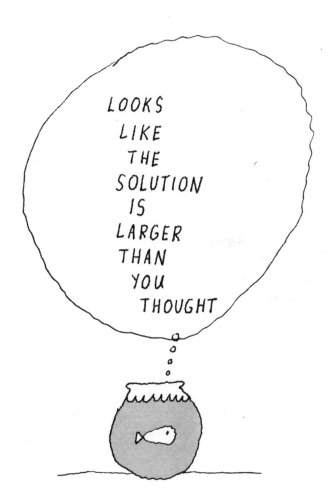

SOME (NEW) VOCABULARY

THE IDIOM	BEFORE	AFTER
LOVE SONGS	Vaguely noted on long elevator rides	Now speaking directly to you
PATHETIC FALLACY	I think I remember something about this from high school English class.	Rain is a direct message about how bad you feel.
"LET'S TAKE A BREAK"	A chance to have one more coffee before lunch	The beginning of the end

There is no plan
you can't pretend
to be following

<u>SPORTS METAPHORS!</u>

KNOCKOUT
STRIKING OUT
HARDBALL
BIG GAME OF LIFE .
PLAYING THE FEILD
IN THE RING

(UM , NEVERMIND . MAYBE SPORTS
CAN'T REALLY HELP NOW.)

GETTING
A DOG
DOESN'T
NECESSARILY
MEAN YOU
HAVE MOVED
ON ...

AND PARTICULARLY
NOT IF
YOU GIVE IT
THE NAME
YOU HAD PICKED
FOR THE BABY.

HELP FROM THE ANIMAL KINGDOM

why not choose a coping strategy
INSPIRED BY NATURE?

WORM

• can live with the split

THE TURTLE

• self-reliant,
well protected,
hard to read

SQUIRREL

• a planner

CAT

• not really known
for loyalty

BIRD

• generally considers
itself free
• partial to the long
winter vacation

Let's make

A CAESAR SALAD (with just a hint of remorse)

AN EGG
(I think)

ONE HEAD
OF CRISP, FRESH
ROMAINE LETTUCE
(gently torn)

JUST A
HINT OF
ANCHOVY
PASTE

BLACK PEPPER —
he always used
a lot

A FINE PARMIGIANO-
REGGIANO CHEESE
FROM THAT
LITTLE PLACE
WE DISCOVERED

NOW WHAT WAS
THAT LAST INGREDIEN
SOMETHING ONLY
HE KNEW ABOUT
SHOULD I CALL?
GOD, WHY
AM I
ALONE?

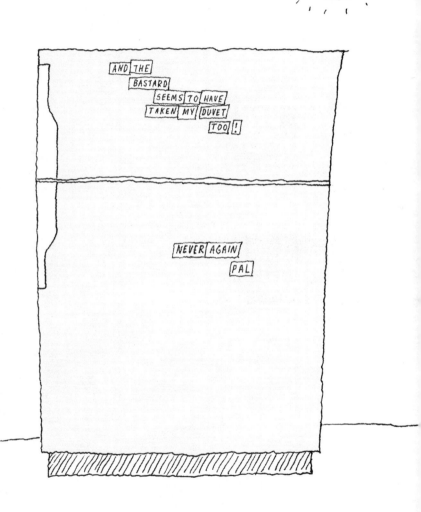

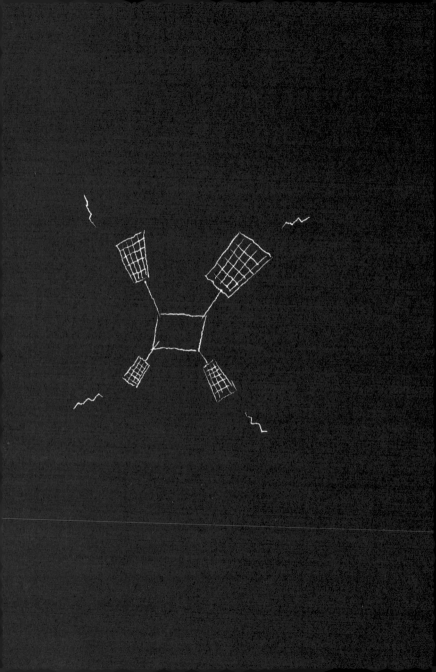

sends out a signal

gets nothing in return

1. SHANNON SAYS SHE IS ELEVEN MONTHS PREGNANT BY DAN.

2. DAN ADMITS HE CHEATED ON HER WITH HER BEST FRIEND.

3. MEANWHILE, TONY IS IN A LOVE TRIANGLE WITH SELA.

4. MY WOMAN LOOKS LIKE A MAN.

TELEVISION OFFERS LITTLE SOLACE

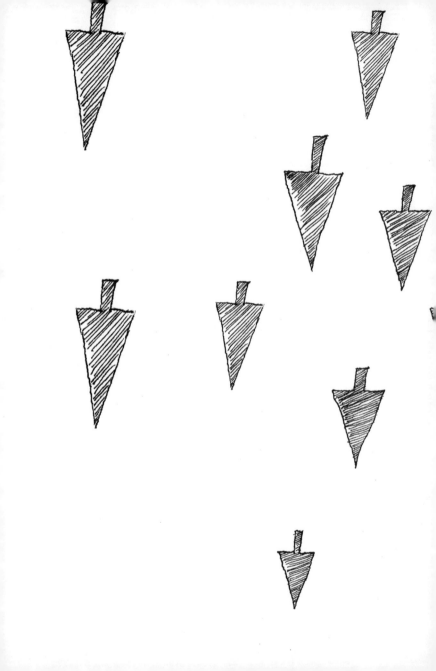

THE CHRISTMAS
DEPRESSION
(c. 1997)

A NOTE ON WINTER

WHILE EACH SNOWFLAKE <u>IS</u>
DIFFERENT, THERE IS SOMETHING
ABOUT LOOKING AT A WHOLE BUNCH
REALLY CAREFULLY THAT MAKES YOU
FEEL LIKE MAYBE YOU ARE SPENDING
A LITTLE TOO MUCH TIME ALONE.

FESTIVE ACTIVITY FOR
THE LONELY:

EAVE MILK AND COOKIES OUT FOR YOURSELF.

finish

start over again

YOU HAVE COME
TO UNDERSTAND
WHALE SONGS
WHILE LYING IN BED.

Your Third Encounter

A SMALL WAVE
OF REMORSE

TWO FALSE EYELASHES

TWO REAL TEARS

SHE

SEEMS TO REQUIRE
SOMETHING YOU NEVER
REALLY HAD

--- --- --- --- --- --- --- --- --- --- ---

HE

HAS BEEN SPENDING
A LOT OF TIME AT
THE TACO VILLAGE

GETTING ADVICE

Here are some people who, while offering new metaphors, can do little to actually help you with what went wrong.

CARDS FOR THOSE AWKWARD MOMENTS

SORRY
I
BROKE
UP
WITH
YOUR
CHILD

Merry Christmas anyway

Season's Greetings

*no,
I'll never be
your
son - in - law.*

Sorry.

THE EVENING

☐ DISASTROUS

☐ MELANCHOLIC

☐ NO WORSE THAN LAST NIGHT

☐ MARBLED WITH SEVERAL MOODS

☐ LONGER THAN I NEEDED IT TO BE

THE MORNING

☐ SORT OF LIKE LAST NIGHT ONLY BRIGHTER

WINTER ACTIVITY FOR THE LONELY:

THROW A SNOWBALL AT YOURSELF.

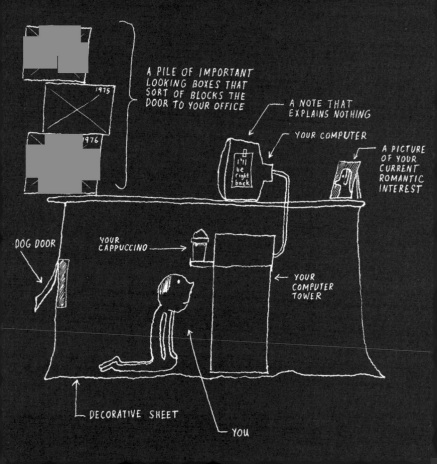

SMALL PLEASURES

<u>STUMBLING ACTIVITY</u>

1. CLOSE YOUR EYES.

2. JUST KEEP THEM CLOSED.

CONSIDERING A NEW HOBBY?

why not try a little gardening

DEMANDS LITTLE,
    GIVES LITTLE IN RETURN,

GETTING CLOSURE

LITTLE HELP FROM YOUR FRIENDS

MORE DUBIOUS CHOICES

FOR YOUR WALLET

~ *Officially Single* ~

CARD

NAME: _____

MEMBER SINCE: _____

YOU ARE FINDING
IT HARD TO GET THE
PHRASE "SO WRONG
IT'S RIGHT" OUT OF
YOUR HEAD.

Your Fourth Encounter

SPRING ACTIVITY FOR THE LONELY:

GARDENING

SHE WAS NEVER REALLY

○ CERTAIN
○ UNCERTAIN
○ PALE
○ WAITING
○ ANY OF THE ABOVE .

SOMETIMES

KNOWLEDGE ≠ POWER

IT'S THE LITTLE THINGS
THAT MAKE YOU LOSE IT

SEPARATED FROM
ITS MATCHER
SOME TIME AGO

Let's COMPARE

THE GREAT DEPRESSION

MY DEPRESSION

LAST NIGHT

I SLEPT LIKE
A BABY
IN THE SENSE
THAT I WOKE UP
EVERY TWO
HOURS SCREAMING
FOR MY MOMMY

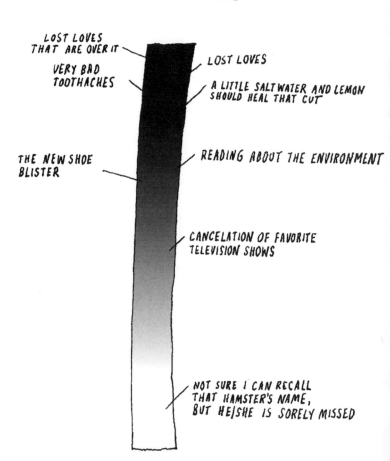

MAPPING

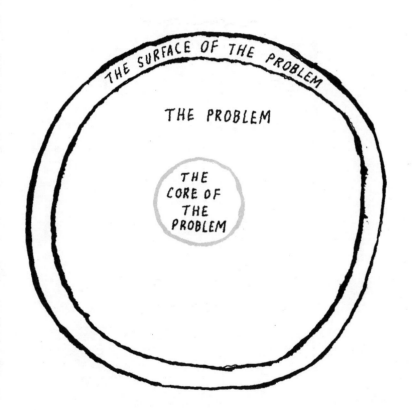

THE SURFACE OF THE PROBLEM

THE PROBLEM

THE CORE OF THE PROBLEM

SOMETIMES THERE ARE NO TWO WAYS
AROUND IT

IT SEEMS THAT THIS GLASS IS
COMPLETELY EMPTY

AUTO RESPONSE

THE RECEIVER OF
YOUR RECENT MESSAGE
HAS PRETTY MUCH
STOPPED COMMUNICATION
WITH THE OUTSIDE
WORLD.

⚠ NO ATTACHMENTS

SLEEPING ALONE

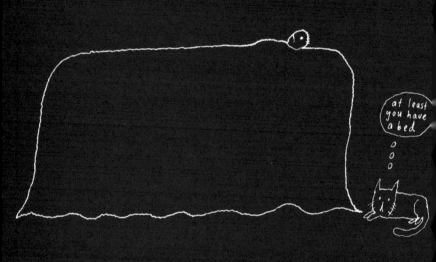

at least you have a bed

* BED SHOWN PSYCHOLOGICALLY TO SCALE

<u>BETWEEN</u>

1. SPEND ALL DAY IN BED.

2. TELL PEOPLE YOU ARE
   BETWEEN PROJECTS.

new projects that make you

SOUND LIKE YOU ARE OVER IT

send the RIGHT message

GOOD	IFFY	NOT SO GOOD
Building a house	Working on my novel	Thinking of becoming a waiter
Joined Doctors Without Borders	Going back to school	Going back to sleep
Dating an astrophysicist mountain climber	Trying to date	Really talking with the cat
Teaching SCUBA diving in Peru	Freelancing	Spending a lot of time in chat rooms
Sold my screenplay	Constructing a time machine	My parents have promised me my old room back
Training in Tuscan cooking near Florence	Really liking Greg, from China Fun delivery	Haven't eaten in days

IN VAIN,

YOU TRY TO RID THE
SODA OF BUBBLES.

YOUR DOG HAS BEGUN TO COMMUNICATE MORE
THAN JUST THE NEED TO VISIT THE PARK

PSYCHOLOGICAL TRIGGERS

ARE NORMALLY INCONSEQUENTIAL OCCURRENCES BECOMING A SOURCE OF GREAT PAIN? HOW MANY OF THESE SET YOU OFF?

- [ ] MOST HOLIDAYS, AND PARTICULARLY OPENING UP THE BOX OF CHRISTMAS DECORATIONS FROM A FEW YEARS BACK

- [ ] RETURNING FROM THE AIRPORT ALONE

- [ ] STUFFED ANIMALS THAT SEEM NEEDLESSLY HAPPY

- [ ] THE SOUND OF MAIL BEING DELIVERED TO YOUR NEIGHBORS

- [ ] EVEN A CURSORY LOOK AT YOUR BED

- [ ] SEASONS CHANGING

- [ ] YOUR PHOTO ALBUMS ... JUST THE FACT THAT THEY EXIST SOMEWHERE

- [ ] OTHER PEOPLE'S PHOTO ALBUMS

$\boxed{\text{KEY}}$

① A coat gives the appearance that you are waiting for someone who is just about to show up.

② A flask of Scotch goes quite nicely with the buttery popcorn.

③ Those perfume ads are mildly sexy — I think Beyoncé is into me.

④ Escaping into other people's problems just kind of cheers a person up.

⑤ The darkness can be consoling.

⑥ You are allowed to cry.

look, it's a BUMPER STICKER

WE GOT ½ WAY THERE

WHAT WENT WRONG IN BED
(I THINK)

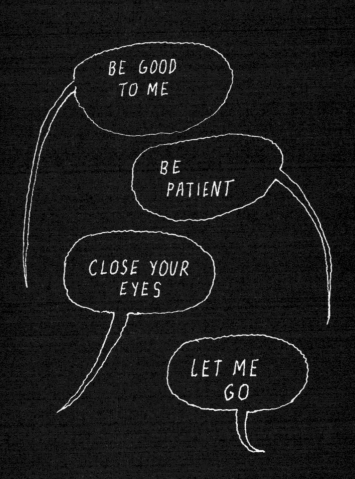

FIFTEEN MOODS

from last winter

VALENTINY

"♡

Looking for something a little more PERSONALIZED this Valentine's Day? Why not say exactly what you mean with a HOMEMADE card.

I HAVE A FEELING THAT THIS'LL BE THE LAST VALENTINE I SEND YOU

YES, I DO LOVE YOU

BUT NOT QUITE IN THE SAME WAY AS BEFORE. YOU KNOW WHEN PEOPLE SAY THEY "LOVE" PASTA PRIMA-VERA, WELL IT'S KIND OF LIKE THAT.

I don't have a clue what is going on in this relationship

are we still going out?

I love your cousin

COUNTRY WOMAN

please
do not
go and
leave my

sorry ass

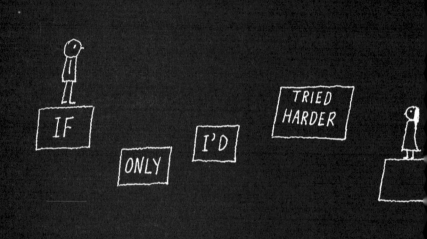

(some) BAND-AID® SOLUTIONS

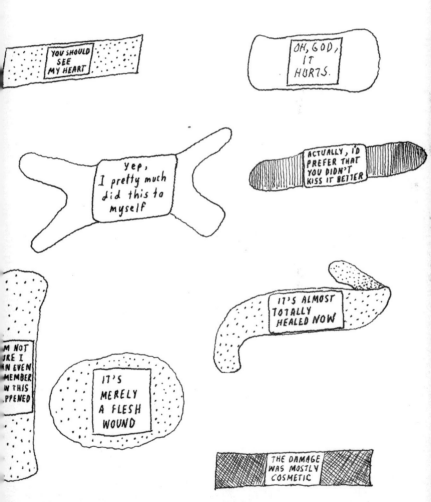

The
Stuff

THE SHARED PET

SHE MUST HAVE STRUCK A DEAL WITH
THE CAT, WHO SHOWS NO INTEREST ANYMORE.

REUNION

1. GATHER YOUR THINGS TOGETHER.
2. CALL IT A REUNION.

WARNING:

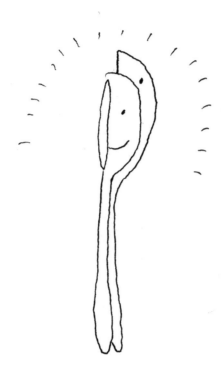

THE APPARENT COMPATIBILITY OF COMMON
HOUSEHOLD OBJECTS MAY NOW MAKE YOU
WISTFUL.

SO SHE IS COMING OVER TO WHAT USED TO BE
YOUR SHARED HOME FOR THE FIRST TIME SINCE
YOU BROKE UP

Let's make a list

1. CLEAN HOUSE

2. PLACE PICTURES OF YOUR NEW FRIENDS
   IN THE OLD PICTURE FRAMES

3. PUT PARTY MIX CD ON

4. SERVE THAT GOURMET FOOD THAT YOU
   KEPT PROMISING IN YOUR OLD RELATIONSHIP

5. HIDE THE VALUABLES FROM THE PAST
   UNDER THE NEW "SPARTAN-LOOK" FURNITURE

6. PLACE HALF-FINISHED CARPENTRY PROJECT
   IN THE CORNER TO SUGGEST NEW AND
   DIFFICULT HOBBY

7. TRY NOT TO BREAK DOWN AND TELL
   HER YOU WANT HER BACK

NOW THAT SHE'S GONE

Let's take a look inside your dresser
at what you still have left

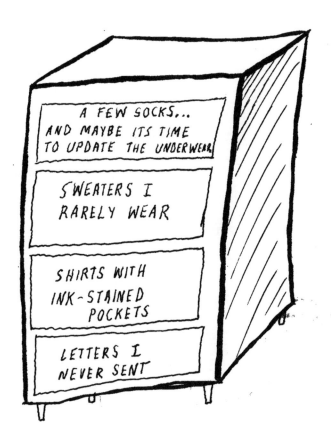

A FEW SOCKS...
AND MAYBE ITS TIME
TO UPDATE THE UNDERWEAR

SWEATERS I
RARELY WEAR

SHIRTS WITH
INK-STAINED
POCKETS

LETTERS I
NEVER SENT

THE EASY LIFE

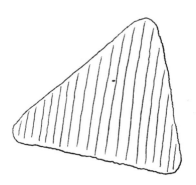

TRY FOODS THAT ARE
ROUGHLY SHAPED TO FIT
YOUR MOUTH, LIKE THIS
HERE TORTILLA CHIP, FOR
EXAMPLE.

A DIET IDEA

1. EAT WHATEVER YOU WANT.

2. TELL PEOPLE YOU ARE FOLLOWING A SPECIAL DIET.

IT SEEMS TO ME THAT

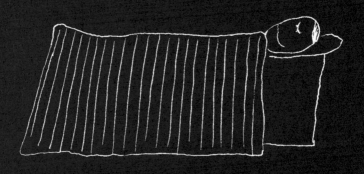

THE SLEEP OF THE JUST IS PRETTY MUCH THE SAME AS THE SLEEP OF THE UNJUST.

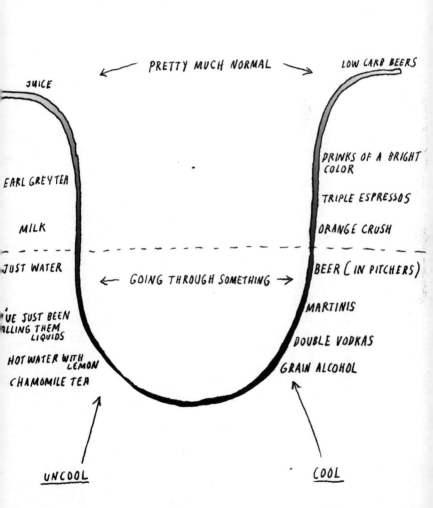

NAVIGATING THE PARTY

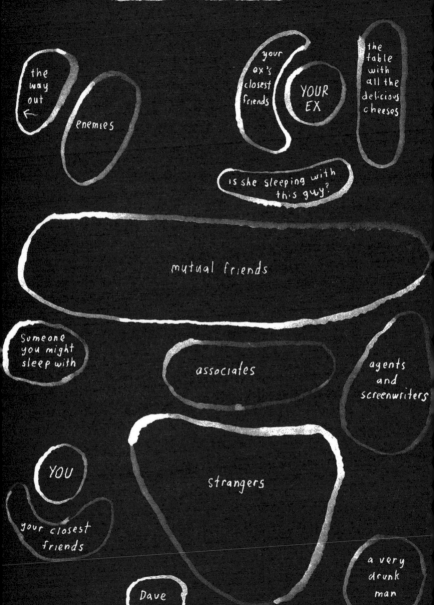

LATELY
THE ONLY STRAWS
YOU ARE GRASPING AT
ARE GOING INTO YOUR
GIN AND TONICS.

SO THE ENGAGEMENT IS OFF

→ WHAT TO DO WITH THE RING ←
(other than sell it)

① FANCY
KEY CHAIN

② SMALL NAPKIN HOLDER

PIZZA+

③ FISHING LURE

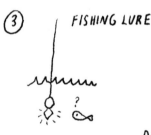

?

④ CONVERSATION PIECE

⑤ DOG TAG

Styles of Communication

PASSIVE

DO A LOT OF
ANGRY THINKING
ABOUT THE
ENGAGEMENT RING

PASSIVE AGGRESSIVE

CASUALLY MENTION
HOW MUCH RINGS
ARE FETCHING ON
eBAY THESE DAYS

AGGRESSIVE

MAIL THE RING
BACK AFTER
TAKING OUT THE
DIAMONDS

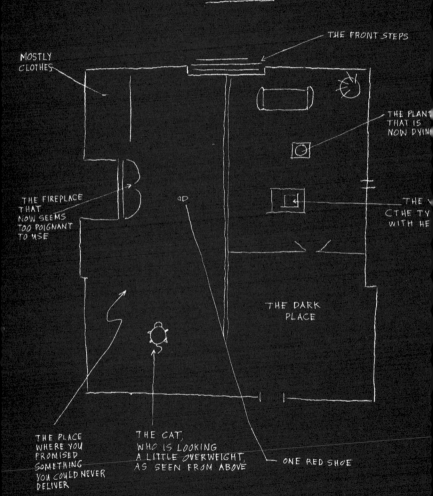

Simple DECORATING ADVICE FOR THE NEWLY SINGLE

MAYBE IT'S TIME TO CONSIDER INVESTING IN A SECTIONAL COUCH

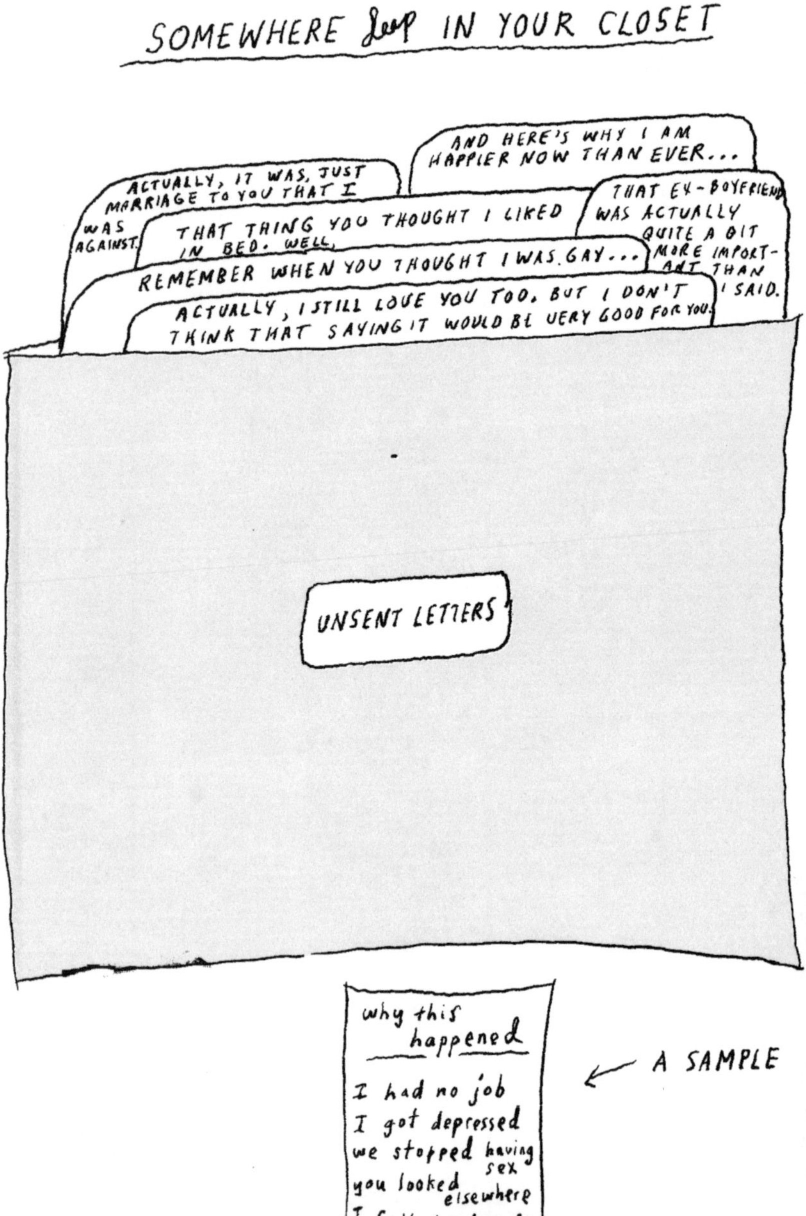
SOMEWHERE deep IN YOUR CLOSET
AND HERE'S WHY I AM HAPPIER NOW THAN EVER...
ACTUALLY, IT WAS, JUST MARRIAGE TO YOU THAT I WAS AGAINST.
THAT EX-BOYFRIEND WAS ACTUALLY QUITE A BIT MORE IMPORTANT THAN I SAID.
THAT THING YOU THOUGHT I LIKED IN BED. WELL,
REMEMBER WHEN YOU THOUGHT I WAS GAY...
ACTUALLY, I STILL LOVE YOU TOO. BUT I DON'T THINK THAT SAYING IT WOULD BE VERY GOOD FOR YOU.
UNSENT LETTERS
why this happened
I had no job
I got depressed
we stopped having sex
you looked elsewhere
I felt abandoned
A SAMPLE

SO FAR TODAY

- ☐ ORGANIZED MY THOUGHTS ABOUT LAST NIGHT'S SLEEP

- ☐ TESTED BOTH SIDES OF THE BED FOR SOFTNESS

- ☐ DID SOME ELECTRICAL WORK ON MY ALARM CLOCK (UNPLUGGING MOSTLY

- ☐ CONSTRUCTED A FORT FOR MYSELF OUT OF PILLOWS AND BLANKETS

- ☐ DEVELOPED A LONG-TERM PLAN FOR ACTUALLY GETTING OUT OF BED

- ☐ MADE THIS LIST

Maybe it's time to

REPHRASE YOUR ANSWERING MACHINE MESSAGE

WE ARE NOT
HERE. IN FACT THERE
IS NO MORE "WE." I AM
FINDING IT DIFFICULT TO GET
OUT OF BED AND ANSWER THE
PHONE AT THE MOMENT.

BUT GO AHEAD AND
LEAVE A MESSAGE.

Bleeep.

Reflexology for the Lonely

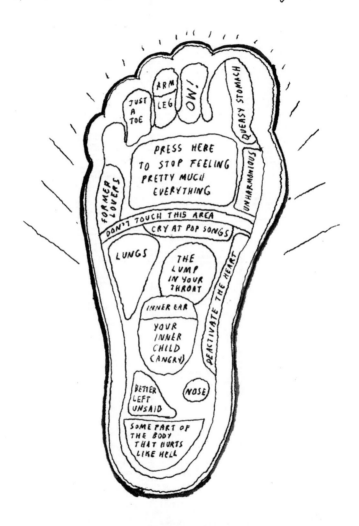

* ALSO TRY O ACUPUNCTURING YOUR EX
O USING CRYSTALS TO CAUSE PAIN
O 'THE WAY' AS IT RELATES TO FINDING A NEW DA

UNDER THE SINK

(some products for the recently broken up)

and IN THE MEDICINE CABINET

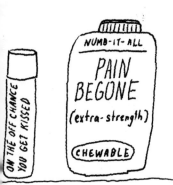

NUMB-IT-ALL

PAIN BEGONE

(extra-strength)

CHEWABLE

ON THE OFF CHANCE YOU GET KISSED

SLEEP and JUST KEEP SLEEPING

DAY-EEZE

sleep comfortably through the day

DAYTIME FULL FACIAL MASK

WHO ARE YOU KIDDING?

DON'T FORGET TO WASH SOAP

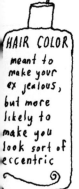

HAIR COLOR meant to make your ex jealous, but more likely to make you look sort of eccentric

deep emotional SCAR REMOVER (and concealer)

OBSESSION

denial

<u>So-so Ideas for your new life</u>

IT IS UNLIKELY
THAT YOUR CAREER
IN FINGER PUPPETRY
WILL EVER REALLY
BE CONSIDERED
GAINFUL EMPLOYMENT

@ ~ You're Invited ~ @

TO THE JOYOUS UNION AND

* WEDDING FOR LIFE *

of

THE PERSON THAT YOU THOUGHT

YOU

would be marrying

(if you can't make it, please
send appropriate presents to us)

P.S.:
HOPE YOU ARE ENJOYING YOUR NEW LIFE,
AND SAY HI TO THE CAT.

AT THE WEDDING

→ Choose a Persona ←

	UNDERSTANDING	OBLIVIOUS	TOUCH OF EVIL	PURE EVIL
THE PERSONA	😊	😐	😏	😈
THE DRINKING	Toast the happy couple	Just don't stop	Why not accidentally spill something on the happy couple	Why not purposely spill something on the happy couple
THE FLIRTING	No	I can't remember	Sleep with the best man, or bridesmaids, or both	The wedding kiss is something you have a right to join in on.
THE OUTFIT	Something like a cardigan	Just wear what you have been sleeping in for the last little while	How about an old picture from your ex's past printed on a T-shirt	Just a tie should be sufficient
THE GIFT	A toaster is always nice	Your old toaster will do	A photo album including some escapades from the past	Well now, lets think this over

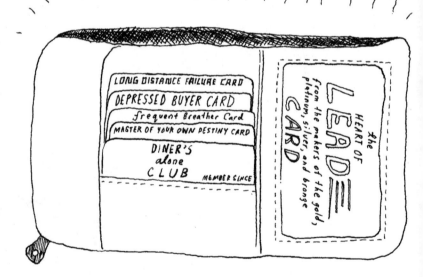

MAYBE A LITTLE MUSIC WILL HELP

A

DANCE TO REMEMBER

B

DANCE TO FORGET

FEEL BETTER.SONGS THAT ARE SO SAD YOU WILL ACTUALLY

Dating

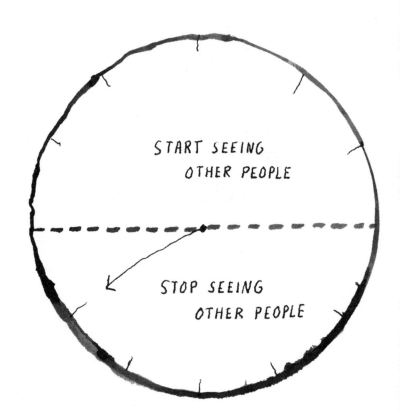

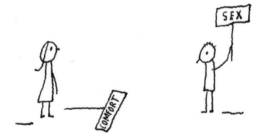

meanwhile

IN THE DATING POOL

Plenty of fish in the sea? How many of these creatures do you recognize?

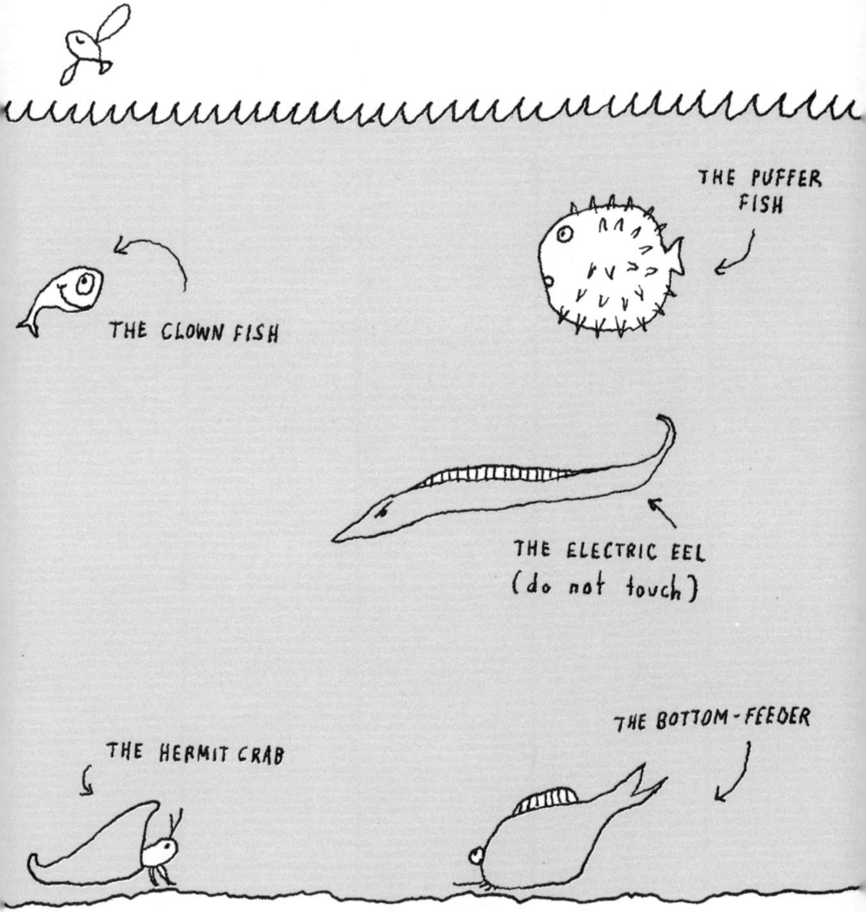

Your Fifth Encounter

FRIENDS AND OTHER PEOPLE YOU MIGHT SLEEP WITH

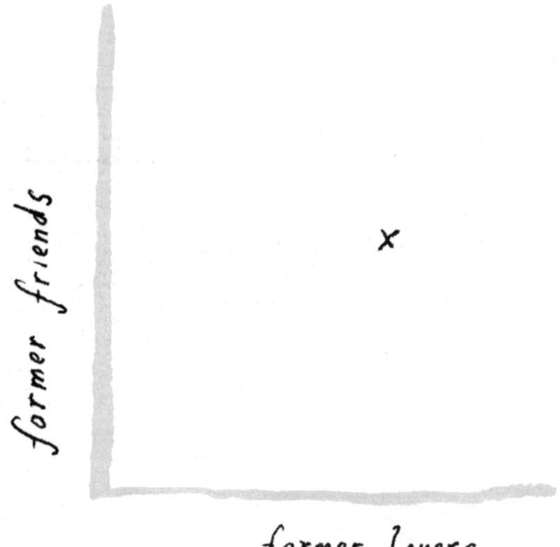

NOT DATING YET?

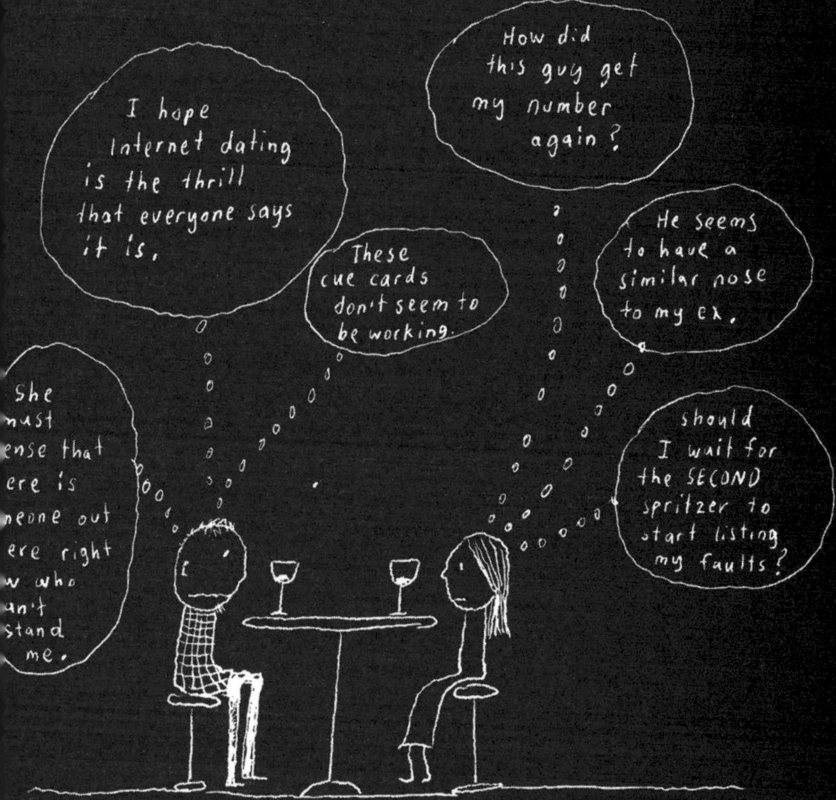

you may be better off

SOME BEER COASTERS TO HELP YOU WITH YOUR CASUAL DATING

Sambuca!

No, I'm not from around here.

WOULD YOU LIKE TO SEE A PICTURE OF MY TROPICAL FISH?

OH, YES
I WILL BE STICKING AROUND FOR LAST CALL.

IF YOU ARE READING THIS Beer Coaster, Perhaps you are as desperate as I am, CAN I BUY YOU A DRINK?

WHY YES, I did produce these scars on my own.

I AM MUTE, BUT WOULD YOU BE WILLING TO GO OUT WITH ME FOR A NIGHT OR TWO?

Please write your name in the space below and while you are At it, let me know if I have even a slim chance
Thanks

Not only is this not my natural hair color, I am not even sure whats left that is natural.

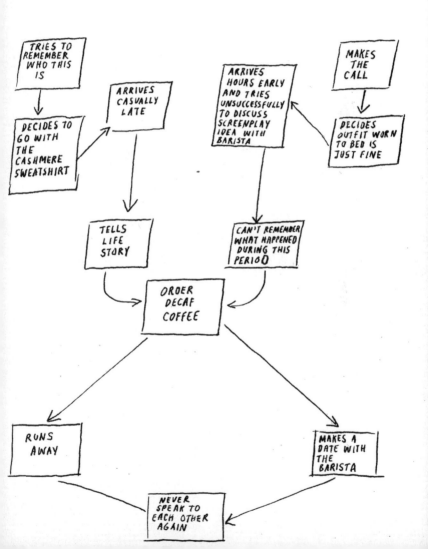

THE UNSPOKEN

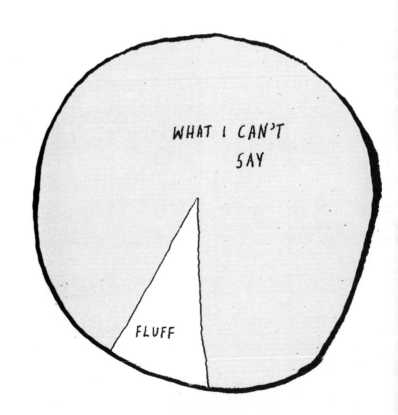

why not <u>REINVENT YOUR BREAKUP</u>
Sometimes wording can make all the difference

(BAD)	(BETTER)
I RAN.	WE SORT OF DRIFTED APART.
I HAD AN AFFAIR.	I NEEDED MORE FREEDOM TO EXPRESS MYSELF IN NEW WAYS.
WE GOT SO BORED THAT FINALLY ALL WE COULD TALK ABOUT WAS TV.	IT WAS FATE.
STOPPED TRYING.	IT'S A MYSTERY TO ME.
THE IRRITATION BECAME TOO MUCH.	IT WAS MUTUAL.

Looking for first date conversation material?
TRY THESE <u>HANDY</u> CUE CARDS

(Conversation Starters)

THE WINE

- REGIONS YOU HAVE VISITED, THAT HINT OF CITRUS AND CASSIS

THE WEATHER

- HOW A STORM CAN MAKE YOU FEEL REALLY ALIVE

FRIENDS

- THE NICE THINGS MUTUAL ACQUAINTANCES HAVE SAID ABOUT YOUR DATE

(Conversation Stoppers)

THE WINE

- YOUR ONGOING BATTLE WITH ALCOHOLISM

THE WEATHER

- HOW MUCH YOU LOVE YOUR BASEMENT APARTMENT FOR BLOCKING ALL NATURAL LIGHT

FRIENDS

- THAT CRAZY NIGHT YOU SPENT WITH YOUR EX'S BEST FRIEND

EXPOSING YOUR INNER SELF

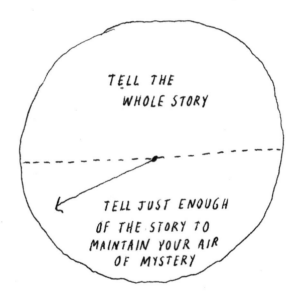

TELL THE
WHOLE STORY

TELL JUST ENOUGH
OF THE STORY TO
MAINTAIN YOUR AIR
OF MYSTERY

MEASURING

TRUE   THE GRAY AREA   FALSE

A DIAGRAM SHOULD MAKE THINGS CLEAR

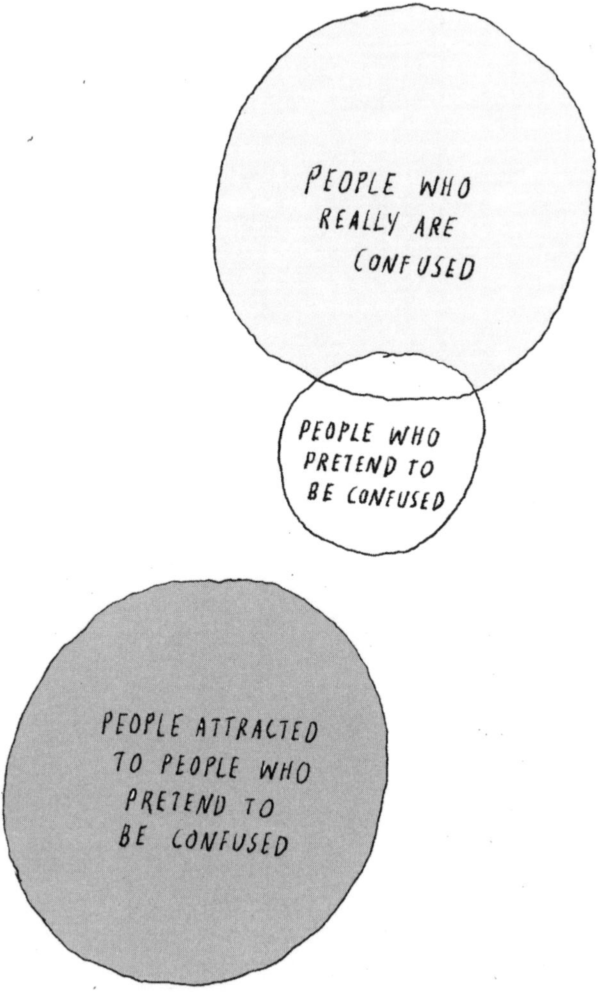

HE SAID / SHE SAID

*

— you're from outer space, she said,

— Everything is from outer space, I said,

(Let's use the telephone)

THE * KEY

* 84	CALL BLOCK
* 76	CALL RETURN
* 61	CALL ERASE
* 43	CALL HOPELESSLY

CONSTRUCT A THEORY!

1. THINK OF SOMETHING.

2. START TELLING PEOPLE
   IT IS YOUR THEORY.

IMAGINARY PARTNER

1. CHOOSE A PERSON ACROSS FROM YOU ON THE SUBWAY TRAIN TO BE YOUR IMAGINARY PARTNER.

2. CHOOSE A CUTE PET NAME FOR YOUR NEW PARTNER.

3. IMAGINE THE SORT OF WORDLESS SCOLDING YOU WILL GET WHEN YOU USE THIS PET NAME IN FRONT OF YOUR PARTNER'S COLLEAGUES.

4. MAYBE WE SHOULD TRY ANOTHER VISUALIZATION EXERCISE. I DON'T THINK THIS ONE IS REALLY WORKING OUT FOR YOU.

NOT QUITE OVER IT? WHY NOT TRY

ANGRY DATING...

date people who look vaguely like your ex

start crying in the middle of the date

a restaurant near your ex's apartment is a wise choice

talk mostly about your ex

wear that sweater your ex gave you

celebrities, models, surfers, and the too young for you make good choices

try to date someone that your ex will later hear about

and as long as you're in the neighbourhood maybe the two of you should just stroll by

watch out that your date is not an angry dater

also try to date people that you swore you were never interested in

So you're a little drunk, why not
e-mail him right now? He'd probably
LOVE to hear about your new relationship.

I'M AFRAID
HE WAS
UNEXPECTEDLY GOOD
IN BED .

OH

YOUR BLIND DATE IS ACTUALLY BLIND

ONE MORE BEER COASTER

WHY YES,

I AM LOOKING
FOR A
SHORTCUT
AROUND
THE PAIN.

MAINTAIN A SPACE CUSHION

TRY TO KEEP AT LEAST ONE PERSON-LENGTH
BETWEEN YOU FOR EVERY YEAR THAT YOU WERE TOGETHER.
(DOUBLE THIS IF YOUR EX SEEMS TO BE WITH SOMEONE NEW.)

HAVE YOU TRIED

Wearing your Breakup?

SO SCRUFFY, IT'S HIP.

VERY DARK, VERY BIG SUNGLASSES

Always good

THE UNWASHED FACE

Be careful with this one — it takes a certain something to really pull off.

THE AMBIGUOUS SMILE

Popular with rock stars and philosophers

THE FUZZY BATHROBE

Prada is considering this look for next season or maybe the season after next.

CIGARETTE

The supermodels seem happy smoking, why shouldn't you?

<u>GOING SLEAZY</u>

(you're on your own.)

why not try to SCARE HER OFF

with the HAGGARD SEA CAPTAIN LOOK

TRY THE
BACK DOOR —
THIS DATE
LOOKS LIKE
IT'S ONLY
GOING TO GET
WORSE.

* FOR THE BATHROOM STALL.
PHOTOCOPY AS NECESSARY.

Your Sixth Encounter

WELL HE _LOOKED_ LIKE DATING MATERIAL

- ☑ SWIMMER'S BODY
- ☑ GOOD CD COLLECTION
- ☑ VERY RICH , BUT SLIGHTLY HIPPIE PARENTS
- ☑ SEEMS TO TAKE TO MY CAT
- ☑ A WELL-WORN TOOL BOX BESIDE HIS SHELF OF OBSCURE POETRY
- ☑ SEEMS TO HAVE A HELICOPTER PILOT'S LICENSE IN HIS WALLET
- ☒ UNFORTUNATELY, HE'S AN ACTOR

WHY NOT TELL
PEOPLE
YOU HAVE A

Canadian Lover

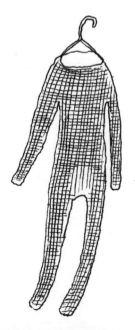

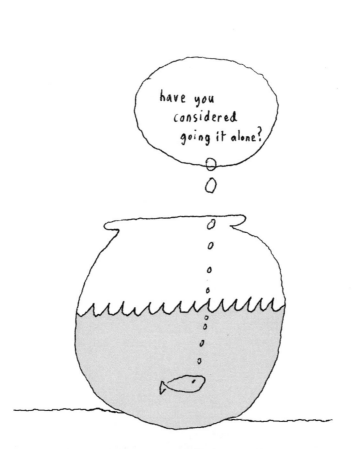

A New Beginning

MOMENTS

I COULD SLEEP WITH

1. ———————————
2. ———————————
3. ———————————

(FOR THE REST OF MY LIFE)

SELF RELIANCE

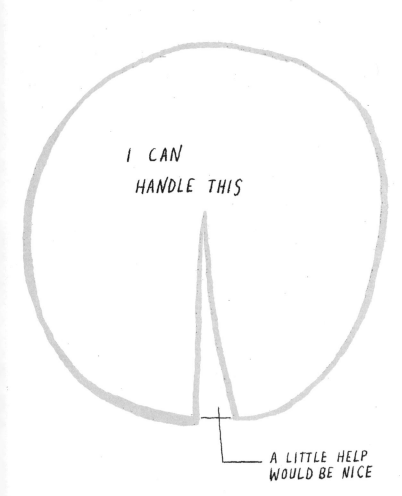

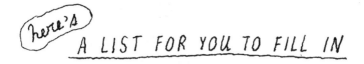

here's A LIST FOR YOU TO FILL IN

THINGS THAT
REMIND YOU
OF HIM IN
THE GOOD WAY

THINGS THAT
REMIND YOU
OF HIM IN
THE BAD WAY

YOU HAVE MOVED FROM
PRETENDING TO BE HAPPY
TO PRETENDING TO BE UNHAPPY.

ANATOMY of the NORMAL HEART

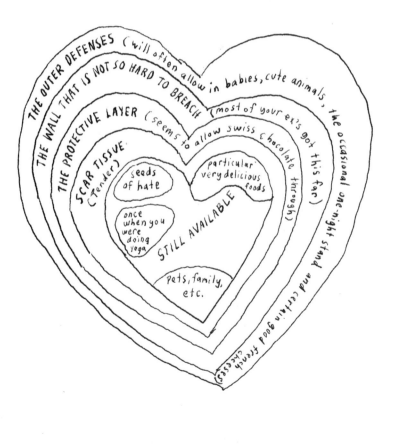

ARE YOU READY FOR LOVE?

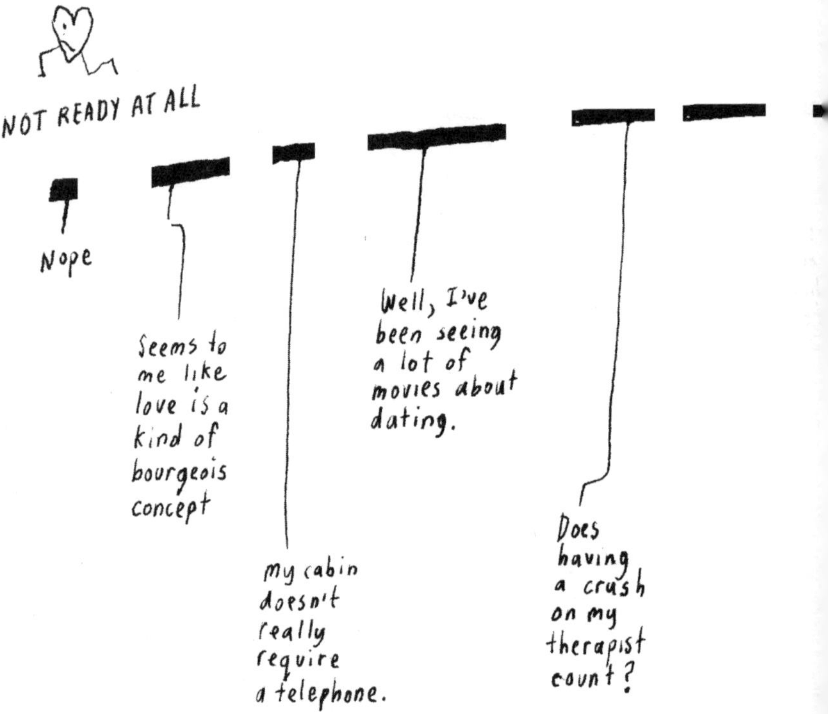

ALMOST
OVERLY READY

I HAVE
begun to
brush my
teeth again.

what about
love of small
animals?

Even the
Ex is
suggesting
I start
dating
again.

I'm spending
a lot of time
in bookstores
looking around
wistfully.

I'm dining
alone by
candlelight.

My cat is
starting to
feel suffo-
cated
by my
affections.

SUMMER ACTIVITY FOR THE LONELY:

THE *RING TOSS*

SUSPECT YOU MIGHT BE ON THE MEND?

Let's have a look around your house
for signs of new life

IN THE KITCHEN

The salt and pepper are no longer alone on your spice rack.

AROUND BACK

Even common weeds seem infused with a kind of zest for life.

IN THE BEDROOM

The bed has become a means to an end rather than an end
unto itself.

IN THE WOODSHOP

Listen, if you have a woodshop you are using, you probably
don't need any help.

SECRET ACTIVITY

1. DO SOMETHING EXTRAORDINARY.

2. TELL NO ONE.

PROMISING

I WILL ONLY DO THAT

☐ ON HALLOWEEN

☐ ON NEWYEAR'S

☐ WHEN I AM REALLY DRUNK

YOU ARE LEARNING
WHAT YOU LIKE BY
TRYING THINGS THAT
YOU DON'T LIKE.

SICKNESS ACTIVITY

1. FIND SOMEONE YOU LOVE.

2. GET HIM OR HER TO MEASURE
   YOUR TEMPERATURE.

FRONTIER ACTIVITY

GO SOMEPLACE
YOU HAVE NEVER BEEN

I WILL

☐ BUY THE CEREAL

☐ TELEPHONE IF I AM
STAYING OUT LATE

☐ ADMIT MY COMPLETE
DEPENDENCE ON YOU

REMEMBER   FORGET

YOUR FUTURE HAPPINESS

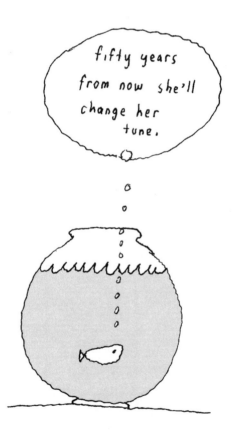

I WILL NEVER STOP BUYING
YOU CLOTHES IN BEAUTIFUL
COLORS YOU WILL NEVER WEAR

Signed: _____
Dated: _____

The Four-Step Process Away from the Vegetarianism That Was Never Your Idea in the First Place

① START ADDING SHAKE 'N BAKE® COATING TO YOUR TOFU

② DECIDE THAT POULTRY IS NOT EXACTLY AN ANIMAL.

③ RECOGNIZE THAT WHILE FISH DO HAVE FEELINGS, THOSE FEELINGS ARE NOT REALLY THAT INTERESTING.

④ IT'S OKAY TO EAT BACON AGAIN. YOU ARE MAKING YOUR OWN RULES NOW.

I WILL

☐ PROTECT YOU FROM DANGER

☐ SPLIT THE ENGLISH MUFFINS

YOU WILL

☐ COME TO MY AID

☐ ASSEMBLE THE FURNITURE

Lingering Doubts

YEARS LATER, HAVING ALREADY MOVED ON TO A NEW RELATIONSHIP, YOU WONDER...

ADMIT ONE
MISTAKE

THANK YOU

DUFF MCDONALD

YOKO ONO

GRAHAM ROUMIEU

SUZANNE SOPINKA

UMA THURMAN

and especially

TRICIA BOCZKOWSKI